BASEBALL'S RECORD BREAKERS

BY HANS HETRICK

CAPSTONE PRESS
a capstone imprint

Sports Illustrated Kids Record Breakers is published in 2017
by Capstone Press, 1710 Roe Crest Drive, North Mankato, Minnesota 56003
www.mycapstone.com

Library of Congress Cataloging-in-Publication Data is available on the Library of Congress website.

ISBN 978-1-5157-3760-5 (library binding)
ISBN 978-1-5157-3764-3 (paperback)
ISBN 978-1-5157-3773-5 (eBook PDF)

Editorial Credits: Nick Healy, editor; Veronica Scott, designer; Eric Gohl, media researcher;
Gene Bentdahl, production specialist

Photo Credits
AP Photo: Mark Duncan, 16, Ted Sande, 24; Getty Images: Focus On Sport, 19, Stringer/David Maxwell,
17, Transcendental Graphics, 27, 28; Library of Congress: 7, 12, 22, 23; Newscom: Everett Collection, 6,
KRT/Bud Skinner, 18; Shutterstock: Eugene Onischenko, cover; Sports Illustrated: Andy Hayt, 10, David
E. Klutho, 26, Heinz Kluetmeier, 4, 8, John G. Zimmerman, 20, John Iacono, 11, 21, John D. Hanlon, 9, 29,
Lane Stewart, 14, Walter Iooss Jr., 5, 25

Design Elements: Shutterstock

Printed in the United States of America.
010054S17

TABLE OF CONTENTS

MADE OF IRON

Rookie shortstop Cal Ripken Jr. sat out the second game of the Baltimore Orioles' doubleheader on May 29, 1982. The next day Ripken returned to the lineup. Over the following 16 years, Ripken started 2,632 games in a row for the Orioles. Despite injuries and Major League Baseball's exhausting 162-game season, the Iron Man played on until September 20, 1998, when he finally took a day off.

Before Ripken, New York Yankees legend Lou Gehrig's 2,130 consecutive games played stood as the record for 56 years. Gehrig hit behind Babe Ruth in the 1927 Yankees' deadly "Murderer's Row" batting lineup. While Ruth was a larger-than-life superstar, Gehrig was baseball's modest hero. At the beginning of the 1939 season, Gehrig's speed and coordination suddenly disintegrated. Doctors discovered Gehrig had ALS, an incurable neurological disease. The Iron Horse died just two years later.

Cal Ripken Jr.

Ripken's 2,632 straight games amount to one of baseball's most beloved records. Fans might not be able to throw a smoking fastball or hit a towering home run. But anyone can show up every day and give his or her best, much like the Iron Man and the Iron Horse did.

RECORD BREAKERS

RIPKEN'S 2,632 IS JUST ONE OF BASEBALL'S LEGENDARY NUMBERS. BASEBALL FANS ARE OBSESSED WITH STATS, NUMBERS, RECORDS, AND THE STORIES BEHIND THEM. FANS WATCH THE GAMES AND TRACK THE NUMBERS, HOPING TO WITNESS SOME NEW BASEBALL MAGIC. A RECORD CAN BE BROKEN IN ANY GAME, AND TODAY'S STARS NEVER STOP CHASING STANDARDS SET BY RIPKEN, GEHRIG, RUTH, AND MANY OTHERS.

NL IRON MAN

Steve Garvey holds the National League (NL) record for consecutive games played with 1,201. Garvey's streak stretched from September 3, 1975, until July 29, 1983. Some fans thought his streak might approach Gehrig's record. But Garvey's run came to an abrupt end when he broke his thumb in a collision at home plate.

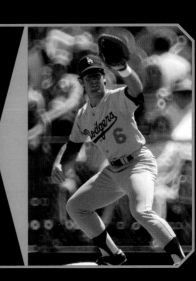

CONSECUTIVE GAMES PLAYED

PLAYER	GAMES	BEGAN	ENDED
Cal Ripken, Jr. (Orioles)	2,632	05-30-1982	09-19-1998
Lou Gehrig (Yankees)	2,130	06-01-1925	04-30-1939
Everett Scott (Red Sox, Yankees)	1,307	06-20-1916	05-05-1925
Steve Garvey (Dodgers, Padres)	1,207	09-03-1975	07-29-1983
Miguel Tejada (A's, Orioles)	1,152	06-01-2000	06-21-2007

Serious baseball fans know the magical number 56. That's because in 1941 Joe DiMaggio, the New York Yankees' legendary centerfielder, recorded a hit in 56 consecutive baseball games. DiMaggio's batting numbers during his streak were stunning. He hit for a .408 average with 15 home runs and 55 runs batted in during those 56 games. He faced four future Hall-of-Fame pitchers and struck out only five times. And DiMaggio would have reached 57 if he hadn't been robbed of hits on two incredible backhanded plays by Cleveland third baseman Ken Keltner.

No player has come within 10 games of DiMaggio's 56. In 1978 Pete Rose hit safely in 44 straight games. Paul Molitor had a great streak of 39 with the Milwaukee Brewers in 1987. And Philadelphia Phillies teammates Jimmy Rollins and Chase Utley reached 38 and 35, respectively, in 2006.

Many experts consider DiMaggio's 56 to be unbreakable, especially in the Major Leagues today. In DiMaggio's era, pitchers typically pitched the entire game. Batters faced the same pitcher four or five times each game. They became familiar with the pitchers' stuff and their approach. Batting averages increased in the late innings. Today it's not unusual for batters to face three or more pitchers in one game.

Joe DiMaggio

Even if conditions favored hitters in his time, DiMaggio's 56 is remarkable. DiMaggio broke Wee Willie Keeler's 44-year-old record of 45 by a whopping 11 games. In the decades since then, no other player has topped Keeler's total, much less gotten a sniff of the record.

Willie Keeler

JOLTIN' JOE

Less than a month after DiMaggio's 56-game hitting streak ended, Les Brown and his orchestra recorded a song called "Joltin' Joe DiMaggio." The song lyrics recounted the hitting streak with big band flair. The song became a hit in 1941, and it's still a fan favorite today.

LONGEST HITTING STREAKS

PLAYER	GAMES	YEAR(S)
1. Joe DiMaggio (Yankees)	56	1941
2. Willie Keeler (Orioles)	45	1896-1897
3. Pete Rose (Reds)	44	1978
4. Bill Dahlen (Colts)	42	1894
5. George Sisler (Browns)	41	1922

MAN OF STEAL

One August night in 1982, Rickey Henderson of the Oakland A's drew a walk in the third inning. He took a lead off of first base, stared intently at Milwaukee Brewers pitcher Doc Medich, and wiggled his fingers. Medich threw over to first base four times trying to pick off Henderson—or at least shorten his lead. Finally, Medich delivered to the plate.

Henderson bolted for second base. In his typical style, he slid headfirst into the base with such force that his helmet flew off. It was close at the bag, but the umpire signaled safe. The play marked Henderson's 119th stolen base of the season, breaking St. Louis Cardinals speedster Lou Brock's record of 118. Henderson stole three more bases that game. By the end of the season, Henderson had swiped 130 bases in all.

Rickey Henderson

Henderson created havoc on the base paths throughout his career. He led the league in steals during 12 seasons. His incredible career landed him in the Hall of Fame. Bill James, a respected baseball historian, celebrated Henderson's achievements by saying, "If you split him in two, you'd have two Hall of Famers."

Henderson possessed a deep love for the game. After his big league career, he continued to play ball for small independent teams such as the Newark Bears and the San Diego SurfDawgs.

RICKEY HENDERSON HOLDS THE RECORD FOR STOLEN BASES IN A CAREER WITH 1,406. NO ONE ELSE HAS TOPPED 1,000 STEALS. HENDERSON SWIPED 468 MORE BASES THAN LOU BROCK, WHO IS SECOND ALL-TIME.

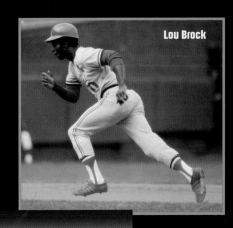

Lou Brock

SINGLE SEASON STEALS (MODERN ERA)

PLAYER	STEALS	YEAR
1. Rickey Henderson (A's)	130	1982
2. Lou Brock (Cardinals)	118	1974
3. Vince Coleman (Cardinals)	110	1985
4. Vince Coleman (Cardinals)	109	1987
5. Rickey Henderson (A's)	108	1983

FASTBALLS FOREVER

Pitching for the Houston Astros, Nolan Ryan topped Walter Johnson's 45-year-old all-time strikeout record on April 27, 1983, in Montreal's Olympic Stadium. Late in the game, Ryan painted the outside corner with a fastball that struck out the Montreal Expos'

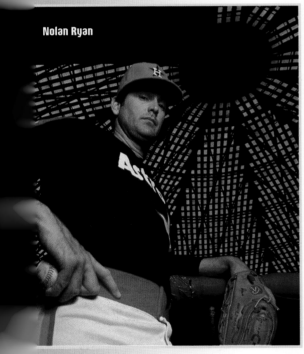

Nolan Ryan

Tim Blackwell swinging, tying Johnson's record at 3,508. For strikeout 3,509, Ryan dropped a backdoor curveball in for a strike to send the next batter down looking.

Ryan earned the nickname "The Ryan Express" because he could throw fastballs at 100 miles per hour. He also kept playing for a long, long time. At age 38 he struck out the New York Mets' Danny Heep for career strikeout number 4,000.

The seemingly ageless Ryan was 42 when he recorded his 5,000th strikeout. That one came against the great Rickey Henderson, who went down swinging on a blazing fastball. Henderson was happy to be a part of the milestone. "It was an honor to be the 5,000th," said Henderson. "As Davey Lopes says, 'If he ain't struck you out, you ain't nobody.'"

Ryan struck out just about everybody in the major leagues, including seven sets of fathers and sons, 12 sets of brothers, and 21 Hall of Famers. When he retired at the age of 46, The Ryan Express had mowed down 5,714 batters.

CAN'T TOUCH THIS

Nolan Ryan tossed an astonishing seven no-hitters during his 27-year career. He threw his first no-hitter at the age of 25 for the California Angels. He threw his seventh no-hitter for the Texas Rangers at the age of 44. Only four other pitchers have thrown more than two no-hitters in the modern era. Dodgers lefty Sandy Koufax tossed four no-hit games. Bob Feller, Larry Corcoran, and Cy Young each threw three no-hitters.

Randy Johnson

CAREER STRIKEOUTS

PLAYER	STRIKEOUTS
Nolan Ryan (Mets, Angels, Astros, Rangers)	5,714
Randy Johnson (Expos, Mariners, Astros, Diamondbacks)	4,875
Roger Clemens (Red Sox, Blue Jays, Yankees, Astros)	4,672
Steve Carlton (Cardinals, Phillies, Giants, White Sox, Indians, Twins)	4,136
Bert Blyleven (Twins, Rangers, Pirates, Indians, Angels)	3,701

THE REAL CY

Every year, sportswriters award the best pitcher in the National League and the best pitcher in the American League with the Cy Young Award. The list of Cy Young Award winners includes legendary pitchers such as Sandy Koufax, Bob Gibson, Randy Johnson, and Greg Maddux. Many fans know all about those players but don't know a thing about the man for whom the award was named.

Cy Young

After having pitched his last game in 1911, Cy Young had clearly set the mark for pitching excellence. Young's 511 career wins, 749 complete games, and 7,356 innings pitched were records unmatched in his day. And they are far beyond the reach of today's pitchers.

Early in his career, Young relied on his magnificent fastball to dominate the big leagues. He started his career with the Cleveland Spiders in 1891. Hall of Famer Cap Anson said that Young's fastball looked as if "the ball was shooting down from the hands of a giant." Young pitched for four other teams and stayed in the game until 1911.

THE WORLD SERIES AS WE KNOW IT TODAY STARTED IN 1903. CY YOUNG THREW THE FIRST PITCH IN WORLD SERIES HISTORY. YOUNG'S BOSTON AMERICANS LOST THAT GAME BUT WON THE SERIES.

Later in his career, Young's fastball lost its spark, but he adapted and turned pitching into an art form. He developed a change-up, a wide array of breaking balls, and different deliveries to fool hitters. "If a right-hander crowded my plate," Young said, "I side-armed him with a curve, and then, when he stepped back, I'd throw an overhand fastball low and outside." Young's strong arm finally gave out at the age of 44, ending the most prolific pitching career in baseball history.

CAREER PITCHING WINS

PLAYER	WINS
1. **Cy Young** (Spiders, Perfectos, Americans, Naps, Rustlers)	511
2. **Walter Johnson** (Senators)	417
3. **Pete Alexander** (Phillies, Cubs, Cardinals)	373
3. **Christy Mathewson** (Giants, Reds)	373
5. **Pud Galvin** (Brown Stockings, Bisons, Alleghenys, Burghers, Pirates, Browns)	365
6. **Warren Spahn** (Braves, Mets, Giants)	363
7. **Kid Nichols** (Beaneaters, Cardinals, Phillies)	361
8. **Greg Maddux** (Cubs, Braves, Dodgers, Padres)	355
9. **Roger Clemens** (Red Sox, Blue Jays, Yankees, Astros)	354
10. **Tim Keefe** (Trojans, Metropolitans, Giants, Phillies)	342

THE HIT KING

Pete Rose's career as a baseball player seemed like a fairy tale. Rose was born and raised a proud kid from Ohio. Although he was unknown to most baseball scouts, his beloved hometown team, the Reds, signed him to an amateur free agent contract in 1960.

The young outfielder wasn't the greatest athlete—neither fast nor graceful. He didn't have a great arm or a powerful bat. But Rose had an incredible eye, a quick bat as a switch hitter, and a knack for figuring out pitchers. He also played hard all of the time. After taking a base on balls, Rose didn't walk to first base—he sprinted. His style earned him the nickname "Charlie Hustle."

Rose broke into the Reds' lineup as a 22-year-old outfielder in 1963. He smacked 170 hits that season and was voted National League Rookie of the Year. In the 1970s Rose played a huge part on Cincinnati's "Big Red Machine" that won two World Series Championships. He won the NL Most Valuable Player award after the 1973 season, and he was World Series MVP in 1975. Reds fans loved their local boy, and Rose loved them back.

Special Year-End Issue

Sports Illustrated

DOUBLE ISSUE   DECEMBER 22–29, 1975   ONE DOLLAR

SPORTSMAN OF THE YEAR: PETE ROSE

Exactly 20 years after getting his first hit, Rose hit safely for the 4,000th time in his career. Rose kept on playing—and hitting. Late in the 1985 season, he laced hit number 4,192 into left center, breaking Ty Cobb's 57-year-old record for most career hits. The sellout crowd at Cincinnati's Riverfront Stadium stood and roared for their hometown hero for seven minutes.

CAREER HITS

PLAYER	SEASONS PLAYED	HITS
1. **Pete Rose** (Reds, Phillies, Expos)	24	4,256
2. **Ty Cobb** (Tigers, A's)	24	4,189
3. **Hank Aaron** (Braves, Brewers)	23	3,771
4. **Stan Musial** (Cardinals)	22	3,630
5. **Tris Speaker** (Red Sox, Indians, Senators, A's)	22	3,514
6. **Derek Jeter** (Yankees)	20	3,465
7. **Cap Anson** (Citys, A's, White Stockings, Colts)	27	3,435
8. **Honus Wagner** (Colonels, Pirates)	21	3,420
9. **Carl Yastrzemski** (Red Sox)	23	3,419
10. **Paul Molitor** (Brewers, Blue Jays, Twins)	21	3,319

PETE ROSE'S FAIRY TALE DIDN'T HAVE A HAPPY ENDING. HE WAS BANNED FROM BASEBALL IN 1989 AFTER BEING INVESTIGATED FOR BETTING ON BASEBALL GAMES WHILE PLAYING AND MANAGING FOR THE REDS. THE BAN MEANS ROSE CANNOT BE CONSIDERED FOR THE BASEBALL HALL OF FAME.

Everyone believed the game was lost for the Cleveland Indians, even Cleveland's players and manager. On August 5, 2001, the Seattle Mariners held a 14-2 lead in the middle innings. Cleveland's manager Charlie Manuel had inserted rookie pitcher Mike Bacsik for mop-up duty and pulled four starters out of the game.

Ken...

Cleveland scored three runs in the bottom of the seventh inning and four runs in the eighth. But nobody got too excited. Seattle still had a comfortable 14-9 lead.

In the bottom of the ninth, though, things got interesting. Cleveland loaded the bases with two outs. Einar Diaz drove in two runs with a single to left field. Seattle manager Lou Piniella brought in closer Kaz Sasaki to slam the door on the rally. Speedster Kenny Lofton promptly singled to load the bases again, sending Omar Vizquel to the plate with his team trailing by three runs. Vizquel ripped a base-clearing triple down the right field line to knot the game at 14.

The teams headed into extra innings, and the Indians finished their impossible comeback victory in the bottom of the eleventh. Lofton sprinted home from second base on a broken-bat single into left field. He slid in safely under the tag at home plate, capping the biggest comeback since 1925.

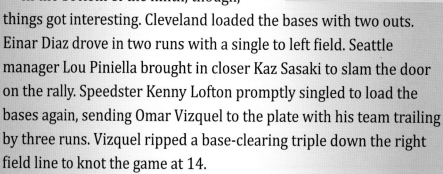

Cleveland's comeback was one of only three 12-run comebacks in baseball's long history. When announcer Jon Miller closed the broadcast, he said, "Well, that may only happen once in a lifetime and maybe even less than that."

MIGHTY MARINERS

Blowing a 12-run lead made for a dark day for the 2001 Mariners, but that season was otherwise full of sunshine. The team won a record 116 games during the regular season, and their outfielder Ichiro Suzuki won the American League Rookie of the Year award.

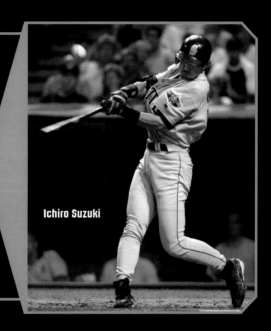

Ichiro Suzuki

MLB'S BIGGEST COMEBACKS

Deficit	Winner	Loser	Date	Final Score
12	Indians	Mariners	August 5, 2001	15-14
12	A's	Indians	June 15, 1925	17-15
12	Tigers	White Sox	June 8, 1911	16-15
11	Phillies	Cubs	April 17, 1976	18-16
11	Cardinals	Giants	June 15, 1952	14-12
11	Astros	Cardinals	July 18, 1994	15-12

THE HOME RUN KING

On April 8, 1974, Hank Aaron drove his 715th home run over the wall in left field. The home run pushed Babe Ruth down to second and propelled Aaron into first on the all-time home run list. When Aaron crossed home plate, his mother was there waiting. "Hammerin' Hank" hugged his mother hard.

Aaron was more relieved than joyful after he broke Ruth's record. A great deal of drama during Aaron's chase to beat Ruth's record occurred off the field. Aaron spent months in the limelight, and some of the attention was downright despicable. Aaron, an African-American, received more than 3,000 letters a day. Many letters were filled with racial hate. Some letters even threatened the life and safety of Aaron, his wife, and his children.

As Aaron closed in on 715, the threats increased. During his chase to become the home run king, he stayed in different hotels under fake names and under the careful watch of bodyguards. It was a miserable experience full of loneliness and fear. But Hammerin' Hank endured and played hard.

Aaron had started his career with the Milwaukee Braves and moved with the team to Atlanta. For his final two seasons, Aaron returned to Milwaukee to play for the Brewers. He retired with 755 career home runs—and the admiration of every real baseball fan.

HANK AARON'S HOME RUN RECORD FELL TO BARRY BONDS AFTER 33 YEARS IN 2007. BONDS HIT 762 HOME RUNS DURING HIS 22-YEAR CAREER. BONDS, HOWEVER, IS AMONG THE PLAYERS WHOSE ACHIEVEMENTS WERE MARRED BY FINDINGS THAT THEY USED PERFORMANCE-ENHANCING DRUGS.

CAREER HRs

PLAYER	MLB SEASONS	HRs
1. **Barry Bonds** (Pirates, Giants)	22	762
2. **Hank Aaron** (Braves, Brewers)	23	755
3. **Babe Ruth** (Red Sox, Yankees, Braves)	22	714
4. **Alex Rodriguez** (Mariners, Rangers, Yankees)	22	696
5. **Willie Mays** (Giants, Mets)	22	660

Sadaharu Oh

HR KINGS

Two of baseball's mightiest batters never played in Major League Baseball. Japan's Sadaharu Oh owns the worldwide professional record for home runs with 868. The legendary Josh Gibson hit an estimated 800 home runs during his career in the Negro Leagues. Gibson's career ended before African-American players were allowed on MLB teams.

SEASONS OF POWER

In the summer of 1961, Roger Maris and Mickey Mantle raced toward Babe Ruth's single-season record of 60 home runs. Maris and Mantle, teammates with the New York Yankees, seemed to match homer for homer. Fans all over the country checked daily sports pages to find out "How many did they get?" Injuries limited Mantle at the end of the year. But Maris continued knocking balls out of the park and broke The Babe's 34-year-old record.

Roger Maris

After 37 years, Maris' record looked ripe to fall during the Great Home Run Race of 1998. Sluggers Mark McGwire of the St. Louis Cardinals and Sammy Sosa of the Chicago Cubs hit home runs at a blistering pace that season. Their dramatic run at the record captured the attention of the nation. Every day, fans watched highlights and again asked, "How many did they get?"

Both Sosa and McGwire passed 61 with weeks yet to play. Sosa finished with 66 home runs, and McGwire set the new record with 70.

Barry Bonds of the San Francisco Giants seized the single-season record on October 5, 2001. Bonds blasted his 71st home run into the right field bleachers in the first inning, passing McGwire for the single-season HR record. Two days later, in the final game of the season, he topped things off with his 73rd home run.

Bonds' record of 73 is epic, but many baseball fans have questioned it. Bonds, McGwire, and Sosa were part of a troubled era in baseball. They and other stars reportedly used performance-enhancing drugs to increase their strength, speed, and endurance. Now many fans wonder if they really were as good as Maris and Ruth.

BARRY BONDS ALSO
HOLDS THE MLB
RECORD FOR WALKS
IN A CAREER
WITH 2,558.

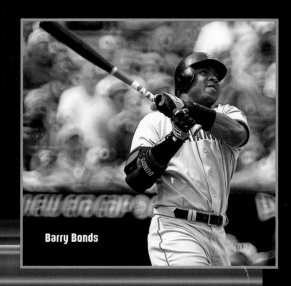

Barry Bonds

SINGLE SEASON HRs

PLAYER	AGE	HRS	SEASON
1. Barry Bonds (Giants)	36	73	2001
2. Mark McGwire (Cardinals)	34	70	1998
3. Sammy Sosa (Cubs)	29	66	1998
4. Mark McGwire (Cardinals)	35	65	1999
5. Sammy Sosa (Cubs)	32	64	2001

JUST PEACHY

Ty Cobb, known as the "Georgia Peach," mastered the art of getting on base. Cobb could slap, poke, and bunt the ball into the empty spots on the field. And he could do those things better than anyone else in the league.

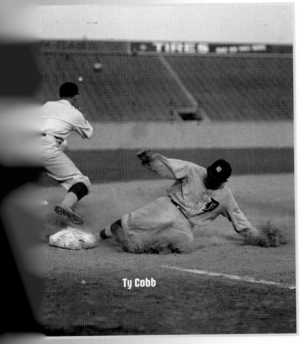

Ty Cobb

No baseball player squeezed more out of the game. Cobb had a habit of kicking the loosely strapped bases. "With each kick, I moved that bag a few inches closer to me," he explained. "After I'd taken my lead, if I had to dive back, that inch or two might be the difference on a pickoff. Never overlook the smallest percentage." Cobb relentlessly practiced nine different types of slides to avoid being tagged out. He used the hook, the fade-away, the straight-ahead, the short or swoop slide, the head-first, the Chicago slide, the first-base slide, the home-plate slide, and the cuttlefish slide. That last one got its name because Cobb sprayed dirt at the fielder like a cuttlefish spurts ink.

When he retired, Cobb owned career records for batting average, stolen bases, hits, and batting titles. His records for career batting average (.366) and batting titles (12) still stand today.

HOW ABOUT A HOMER?

According to legend, Ty Cobb once told a sportswriter, "I'm going for home runs for the first time in my career." That day the 38-year-old hit three home runs. He hit two more the next day, setting a record for home runs in back-to-back games. Cobb quickly returned to his slap hitting style. He finished with 12 home runs that season, matching his career-high.

CAREER BATTING AVERAGE LEADERS

PLAYER	SEASONS	AVERAGE
1. **Ty Cobb** (Tigers, A's)	24	.3664
2. **Rogers Hornsby** (Cardinals, Giants, Braves, Cubs, Browns)	23	.3585
3. **Shoeless Joe Jackson** (A's, Indians, White Sox)	13	.3558
4. **Lefty O'Doul** (Yankees, Red Sox, Giants, Phillies, Dodgers)	11	.3493
5. **Ed Delahanty** (Quakers, Infants, Phillies, Senators)	16	.3458
6. **Tris Speaker** (Red Sox, Indians, Senators, A's)	22	.3447
7. **Billy Hamilton** (Cowboys, Phillies, Beaneaters)	14	.3444
7. **Ted Williams** (Red Sox)	19	.3444
9. **Dan Brouthers** (Trojans, Bisons, Wolverines, Beaneaters, Reds, Grooms, Orioles, Colonels)	19	.3421
9. **Babe Ruth** (Red Sox, Yankees, Braves)	22	.3421

.400 OR BUST

Ted Williams could have sat out the last day of the 1941 baseball season. The Red Sox doubleheader was meaningless because the Yankees had clinched the AL pennant. And Boston Red Sox manager Joe Cronin told Williams he didn't have to play. Williams' batting average was .39955, and, officially, it would have been rounded up, giving him a .400 season. But Williams insisted on playing. He said, "If I'm going to be a .400 hitter, I want more than my toenails on the line."

"Teddy Ballgame," as he was called, went 4-for-5 in the first game. In the second game, he went 2-for-3, raising his final season average to .406. No hitter has hit .400 or better since. In fact, only a handful of hitters have even flirted with .400 since 1941.

In 1980 Kansas City Royals great George Brett spent 14 days above .400 late in the season. Newspapers across the country published a daily "Brett Watch" column to report his progress. With 14 games remaining in the season, Brett fell under .400 and stayed there.

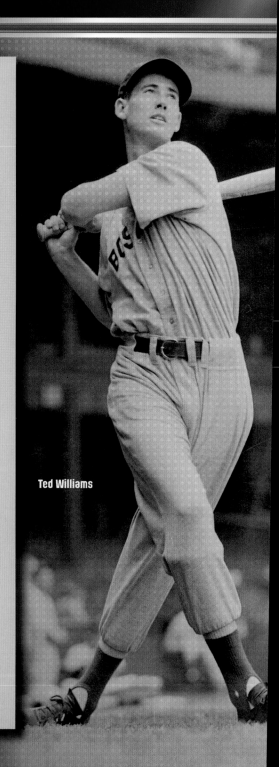

Ted Williams

George Brett

In 1994 Tony Gwynn got hot at the plate, hitting .423 after the All-Star break. Gwynn's average was .394 on August 11th, and he was locked in. But the MLB season halted the next day because of a player strike, and eventually all remaining games were canceled.

Long after he retired, Williams joked, "If I knew that hitting .400 would have been so important, I would have done it more often."

SINGLE SEASON BATTING AVERAGE (MODERN ERA)

PLAYER	SEASON	AVERAGE
1. Nap Lajoie (A's)	1901	.4265
2. Rogers Hornsby (Cardinals)	1924	.4235
3. George Sisler (Browns)	1922	.4198
4. Ty Cobb (Tigers)	1911	.4196
5. Ty Cobb (Tigers)	1912	.4087

HIT MACHINE

Ichiro Suzuki, a transplant from Japan, broke an 84-year-old MLB record in just his fourth year in the league. On October 1, 2004, Ichiro chopped a pitch into the ground and over the head of the third baseman. It was his 257th hit of the year, tying George Sisler's record for single season hits, set in 1920. In the third inning, Ichiro ripped a single up the middle to break the record. And to prove he was one of baseball's greatest hit machines, he hit another single in the sixth.

Ichiro was a throwback to the days of Sisler and Ty Cobb. A surgeon with the bat, Ichiro carved up defenses, directing his hits with a quick flick of his wrists. As a left-handed batter, he jumped out of the batter's box as soon as he made contact. His bat skills, quickness out of the box, and pure speed earned him a tremendous amount of hits.

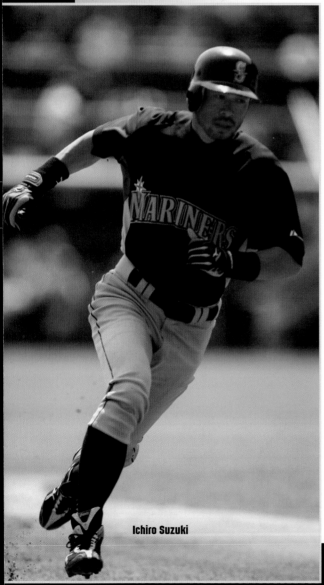

Ichiro Suzuki

Ichiro broke another MLB record by recording more than 200 hits in 10 consecutive seasons. He led the league in hits seven times. And he reminded baseball fans that singles can be nearly as much fun as home runs.

INTERCONTINENTAL HIT KING

Before Ichiro Suzuki played MLB, he recorded 1,278 hits in Japan's Nippon Professional Baseball (NPB) league. In 2016 Ichiro passed Pete Rose for the most hits in professional baseball, if his NPB and MLB hits are added together. At the time Ichiro was 42 years old and in his second season with the Miami Marlins.

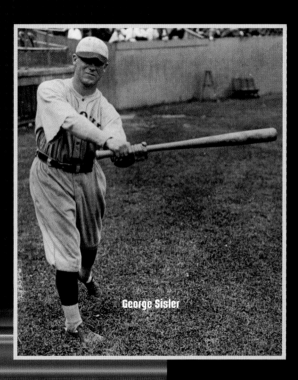
George Sisler

SINGLE SEASON HITS

PLAYER	HITS	SEASON
1. Ichiro Suzuki (Mariners)	262	2004
2. George Sisler (Browns)	257	1920
3. Lefty O'Doul (Phillies)	254	1929
3. Bill Terry (Giants)	254	1930
5. Al Simmons (A's)	253	1925

HEARD 'ROUND THE WORLD

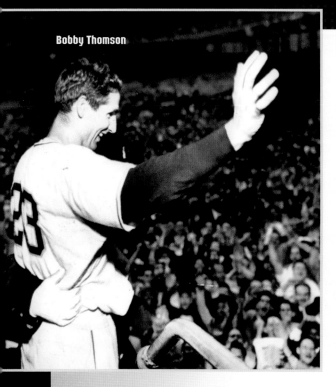

Bobby Thomson

The most famous comeback in a pennant chase ended with Bobby Thomson's dramatic "Shot Heard 'Round the World" home run. In early August 1951, the New York Giants trailed the Brooklyn Dodgers by 13 games. The pennant and a trip to the World Series seemed to be firmly in the Dodgers' grip. The Giants caught fire, however, winning 37 of their last 44 games.

The Giants finished the season tied with the Dodgers. That meant the teams would play a best-of-three series for the National League championship. The Giants won the first game 3-1, but the Dodgers blew them out 10-0 in the second. The third and deciding game was the first sporting event televised live from coast to coast.

The Dodgers broke a 1-1 deadlock with three runs in the eighth inning. In the bottom of the ninth, the Giants strung together two singles and a double to bring the score to 4-2. Then Thomson, an All-Star third baseman, stepped to the plate. He smacked a fastball toward the left field wall, and broadcaster Russ Hodges delivered one of baseball's most famous calls.

"There's a long drive ... it's gonna be, I believe ... The Giants win the pennant!" Hodges yelled. "The Giants win the pennant! The Giants win the pennant! The Giants win the pennant!"

Thomson skipped and hopped around the bases as fans cheered his game-winning three-run homer.

WHEN'S IT OVER?

Baseball's most famous philosopher, Yogi Berra, coined the phrase "It ain't over till it's over" as the manager of the New York Mets. Berra's Mets were 9.5 games behind the Chicago Cubs at the time. Berra proved to be wise. The Mets rallied to clinch the 1973 National League East division title and earn a trip to the postseason.

STRONG DOWN THE STRETCH

These teams came back from the largest gaps to win a division or a pennant.

TEAM	GAMES BEHIND	RECORD	DATE	RECORD AFTER DATE	FINAL RECORD
1914 Braves	15	26-40	July 4	68-19	94-59
1978 Yankees*	14	47-42	July 19	62-21	100-62
1951 Giants **	13	59-51	Aug. 11	38-8	97-59
1995 Mariners	13	43-40	Aug. 2	36-29	79-66
1930 Cardinals	12	53-52	Aug. 8	39-10	92-62
2006 Twins	12	49-40	July 15	47-26	96-66

* won one-game playoff over Red Sox   ** won three-game playoff over Dodgers

GLOSSARY

ALS—amyotrophic lateral sclerosis, also known as Lou Gehrig's disease, is a disease that leads to the loss of control of a person's muscles

breaking ball—a pitch that curves

bunt—when a hitter softly taps a pitch into the infield

change-up—a slow pitch intended to fool the batter

consecutive—in a row, without stopping

lead—the steps taken by a base runner moving toward the next base as the runner awaits the pitcher's delivery

modern era—Major League Baseball after the year 1900, when the rules of baseball were set and since when they have changed very little

no-hitter—a game in which one team doesn't allow the other team to get a hit

penant—in baseball, the prize that is awarded to the champions of the American League and the National League each year

rally—when a team scores more than one run, typically when they are behind in the score

steal—when a baserunner advances to a base to which he is not entitled, most often occurring when the pitcher is delivering a pitch

READ MORE

Braun, Eric. *Baseball Stats and the Stories Behind Them: What Every Fan Needs to Know.* North Mankato, Minn.: Capstone Press, 2014.

Gitlin, Marty. *Baseball Legends in the Making.* North Mankato, Minn.: Capstone Press, 2014.

The Editors of Sports Illustrated Kids. *Baseball: Then to WOW!* New York: Sports Illustrated, 2016.

INTERNET SITES

FactHound offers a safe, fun way to find Internet sites related to this book. All of the sites on FactHound have been researched by our staff.

Here's all you do:
Visit www.facthound.com

Type in this code: 9781515737605

Super-cool stuff! Check out projects, games and lots more at
www.capstonekids.com

INDEX